S0-AAD-537

GUIDE ME IN MY RECOVERY

GUIDE ME

ME

in My

RECOVERY

PRAYERS FOR TIMES OF JOY
AND TIMES OF TRIAL

The Reverend John T. Farrell, Ph.D.

CENTRAL RECOVERY PRESS

CENTRAL RECOVERY PRESS

Central Recovery Press (CRP) is committed to publishing exceptional materials addressing addiction treatment, recovery, and behavioral health care, including original and quality books, audio/visual communications, and Web-based new media. Through a diverse selection of titles, it seeks to impact the behavioral health care field with a broad range of unique resources for professionals, recovering individuals, their families, and the general public. For more information, visit www.centralrecoverypress.com.

Central Recovery Press, Las Vegas, NV 89129
© 2010 by Central Recovery Press
All rights reserved. Published 2010.
Printed in the United States of America.

No part of this publication may be reproduced, stored in a retrieval system, or transmitted in any form or by any means, electronic, mechanical, photocopying, recording, or otherwise, without the written permission of the publisher.

Publisher: Central Recovery Press
            3371 N. Buffalo Drive
            Las Vegas, NV 89129

16 15 14 13 12 11 10   1 2 3 4 5

ISBN-10: 1-936290-02-2 (hardcover)
ISBN-13: 978-1-936290-02-4

The excerpts from Alcoholics Anonymous (AA) are reprinted with permission of Alcoholics Anonymous World Services, Inc. (AAWS) Permission to reprint these excerpts does not mean that AAWS has reviewed or approved the contents of this publication, or that AAWS necessarily agrees with the views expressed herein. AA is a program of recovery from alcoholism only—use of these excerpts in connection with programs and activities that are patterned after AA, but which address other problems, or in any other non-AA context, does not imply otherwise.

Cover design and interior by Sara Streifel, Think Creative Design

This book is dedicated to
Father Henri Nouwen
and Father Mychal Judge,
two spiritual masters
whose paths I can only
hope to follow.

Table of Contents

Acknowledgments

I would like to gratefully acknowledge Stuart Smith who believed I could write this book; Lynne Vittorio who encouraged me; and Nancy Schenck who kept me on task.

Introduction

When initially encountering a program of recovery, many people balk. The reasons for their hesitation are numerous and varied, but often they focus on the spiritual aspects of recovery. Do I have to believe in God? they ask. What kind of God are you talking about? I have a lot of trouble with the God thing, so do I have listen to this stuff? Is the program about religion? What is prayer anyway? What is the point of praying?

Those experienced in recovery, of course, reassure newcomers by explaining to them the difference between religion and spirituality. Religion, we tell them, is about theology and what we believe. Spirituality, on the other hand, is about who we are and how we live. We go on to explain that a successful program of recovery should be about relationships—relationships with God *as we understand* God, a relationship with ourselves, relationships with each other, and relationships with the world around us.

By focusing on right relationships as a foundational part of our recovery, we tell them about connecting with principles, spiritual in nature, which will guide us in our recovery. And we finish by saying that one of the best ways to connect with our spiritual natures—or with our higher power or with our Ground of Being or with our Essence or with God— is to pray.

My own situation in early recovery is a case in point. I grew up in a rule-ridden faith and had long abandoned it. At that point in my life I wasn't especially hostile to spiritual expression. Rather, I was indifferent. I had long since decided that religion, spirituality, and prayer were meaningless to my life. I just couldn't see the point of believing in much of anything besides myself.

As I grew in my recovery, I began to change. I came to understand that a power greater than myself could relieve me of the insanity called the disease of addiction. I began to consider who or what God actually was and what role a higher power played in my recovery. Although I initially encountered the divine as mystery, I eventually came to discern God as the center and the source of goodness and love. As I began to amend my life and form right relationships with those around me and those whom I had harmed, I developed a heightened connectedness to humanity. I also sensed a guiding power or principle that I understood as love and compassion.

At this stage, the poetry of Walt Whitman and John Donne were especially helpful in my growth. It was Whitman who said, "For every atom belonging to me as good belongs to you." John Donne wrote "No man is an island, entire of itself; every man is a piece of the continent, a part of the main; if a clod be washed away by the sea, Europe is the less. . .any man's death diminishes me, because I am involved in mankind."

Their poetical theory of the interconnectedness of humanity enhanced the spiritual healing that was transforming me. Their line of thinking was an antidote to my addictive self who sought isolation, wishing to truly form my own one-person island on the continent of humanity. From Donne, Whitman, and other poets I was able to flesh out the ideas of universal love, ethical behavior, and connectedness that were filling the God-shaped hole in my heart.

But that still left the problem of prayer. Concepts like prayer and meditation hadn't been part of my life during my active addiction. And, as much I hated to admit it, I really had no idea how to pray or what to pray for.

Little did I know I was hardly alone; I had a lot of company in my ignorance.

In fact, the questions of how to pray and why prayer is important have perplexed people—addicts and non-addicts alike—throughout the ages. Spiritual masters have provided us with clues to the answers, but rarely with detailed methods that are applicable for all people at all times. For instance, when Jesus was asked how to pray, he taught his disciples the Our Father. When Mohammed was asked, "Tell us, which action is dearest to Allah?" He answered "To say your prayer at its proper time." Buddha counseled his followers that "The greatest prayer is patience."

Initially, I regarded prayer as something a person did by rote. It never dawned on me that the words of prayers had deep resonance and that those praying the words were to contemplate what they were saying. To illustrate, it wasn't until I started attending meetings that I learned "ourfatherwhoartinheaven" wasn't one word. I'm not sure I had ever heard the Serenity Prayer or the Prayer of St. Francis.

Later on I learned that prayer didn't even have to contain words. One of the useful definitions of prayer for me is the one that explains prayer as responding to God, by thought and by deeds, with or without words. Mahatma Gandhi used to say that prayer is not about asking. Instead, prayer speaks to the soul's deep longings, and in prayer we can admit weakness. Prayer can mean that our hearts speak without words, a condition better than just speaking the words without a heart.

"Prayer is not asking" was a key concept for me. For a long time I assumed that prayer was about asking for specific things or asking for things to happen—a new car to replace the clunker, a better job, a new relationship to replace the one I had lost, winning a game, getting out of trouble, or finding my lost keys. But I learned that more mature prayer was about seeking growth and connection. If I were to "ask" for anything in my prayers, it should be the strengthening of attributes already present, such as patience, humility, comfort, fortitude, etc.

Gandhi wasn't the only person to teach me this lesson. St. Francis was even blunter when he said, "When we pray to God we must be seeking nothing—nothing." The deepest prayer is really about connecting and listening and comes in three steps. First, prayer is about connecting to your spiritual self and its longings. Second, it is about listening to the small, still voice inside of you that is your essence and the source of goodness. And finally, it is about applying whatever you heard (or didn't hear) to form and strengthen your relations with others.

In a way, this book is a prayer. Over the years I have learned through my prayers that the noblest life for me to live is a life of service. I often struggle with service to others as my calling, since by nature I am self-centered, short-tempered, and ungenerous. But recovery and God have a way of getting under one's skin, and as a result, my spiritual progress, while slow, has been perceptible. I have tried to serve others in my personal life, in my professional life, and in my own life of recovery freely and generously. In that process, I have learned much about prayer and maybe something about life. This book is an effort to share some of the wisdom and grace I have gained in my recovery journey. Two awakenings in particular are embedded throughout this book: addiction results from a spiritual vacuum and spirituality fills that vacuum.

To that end, *Guide Me in My Recovery* is an anthology of prayers designed for people in recovery, although recovery is not a requirement to use any or all of these prayers. The book's title is an allusion to the Third Step Prayer found in the recovery text of a twelve-step program. For those of you who might not know, the Twelve Steps are the common denominator of all twelve-step programs of recovery. Step Three proposes that those in recovery make a decision to turn their will and lives over to God or their higher power. I believe the Third Step is so important to placing recovery on a spiritual plane that I have included an entire chapter in *Guide Me in My Recovery* devoted to Third Step prayers. Some of these prayers you may find useful, some eloquent, some familiar, and some off-beat.

In addition to the chapter on Third Step prayers, there are eleven other chapters divided by situations and events that might require the thoughts and words of prayers framed with a particular emphasis.

There are daily prayers and prayers to use when times are joyful and when times are tough. Some of the prayers are famous, some are obscure, and some were written by me. Many of them come from the Christian tradition, but I have included prayers from other faith traditions as well because I believe that God hears all prayers. And for those of you interested in learning more about prayer, I've included a list of recommended sources at the end of the book.

Let me end this Introduction with a prayer before you begin reading.

A Prayer

JANE AUSTEN

Give us grace almighty father, so to pray,
as to deserve to be heard, to address thee with
our hearts, as with our lips. Thou art everywhere
present; from thee no secret can be hid.
May the knowledge of this, teach us to fix our
thoughts on thee, with reverence and devotion
that we pray not in vain. . . .

Give us a thankful sense of the blessings
in which we live, of the many comforts of our lot;
that we may not deserve to lose them by
discontent or indifference. Hear us almighty God,
for his sake who has redeemed us, and taught
us thus to pray. *Amen.*

Morning Prayers

Discipline is a word many people—especially those in recovery—don't like to hear. It smacks of authoritarianism, and we fear it will stifle our independence. It also conjures up memories of being punished when we were young. But these are not the term's only meanings. Spiritually, discipline takes on a far deeper and positive meaning. It is used to mean "training to improve strength or self-control." And in the case of our spiritual lives, the discipline of prayer may be regarded as a holy habit, training to improve our spiritual strength.

One of the most important parts of our daily spiritual discipline should be prayer at regular times during the day. Morning is one of the traditional times to be still and pray. In Psalm 5, for instance, the poet sings, "My voice You shall hear in the morning, O Lord; in the morning will I direct my prayer to You, and will look up." While we have been asleep, God has been working and making changes in all of nature. As we open our eyes, we see and experience light and life coming out of the passivity and darkness of sleep. Refreshed and renewed—resurrected, if you will—we wake up to action.

The prayers in this chapter are all designed to help us start our day with a clear mind and a light heart. They are far-reaching in the types of spiritual traditions from which they are derived. There are ancient Celtic and Scottish prayers, petitions from Native American and African sources, a prayer by Dr. Samuel Johnson, and several joyful hymns. Also included are entries from William Penn, Ralph Waldo Emerson, and a traditional Christian confession to start the day with a clean slate.

A Scottish Morning Prayer

ANONYMOUS

May the blessing of light be on you—
light without and light within.

May the blessed sunlight shine on you
like a great peat fire, so that stranger and
friend may come and warm himself at it.

And may light shine out of the two eyes of you,
like a candle set in the window of a house,
bidding the wanderer come in out of the storm.

And may the blessing of the rain be on you,
may it beat upon your Spirit and wash it fair
and clean, and leave there a shining pool where
the blue of Heaven shines, and sometimes a star.

And may the blessing of the earth be on you,
soft under your feet as you pass along the roads,
soft under you as you lie out on it, tired at the
end of day; and may it rest easy over you when,
at last, you lie out under it.

May it rest so lightly over you that your
soul may be out from under it quickly;
up and off and on its way to God.

And now may the Lord bless you,
and bless you kindly. *Amen.*

Great Spirit Prayer

CHIEF YELLOW LARK OF THE SIOUX

Oh Great Spirit, whose voice I hear in the winds,
whose breath gives life to the world, hear me.

I am small and weak, and I need your strength
and wisdom. May I walk in beauty. Make my eyes
behold the red and purple sunrise;

Make my hands respect the things you have made
and my ears sharp to hear your voice;

Make me wise so that I may know the things you
have taught your children. The lessons you have
written in every leaf and rock;

Make me strong, not to be superior
to my sisters and brothers, but to fight
my greatest enemy within myself;

Make me ready to come to you with straight eyes
so that when my life fades as the fading sunset my
spirit may come to you without shame.

Thanksgiving

RALPH WALDO EMERSON

For each new morning with its light,
For rest and shelter of the night,
For health and food,
For love and friends,
For everything Thy goodness sends.

Morning Confession

Most merciful God,
We confess that we have sinned against you
In thought, word, and deed,
By what we have done,
And by what we have left undone.
We have not loved you with our whole heart;
We have not loved our neighbors as ourselves.
We are truly sorry and we humbly repent.
For the sake of your son Jesus Christ,
Have mercy on us and forgive us;
That we may delight in your will,
And walk in your ways,
To the glory of your name. *Amen.*

You Are the Peace of All Things Calm

CELTIC PRAYER

You are the peace of all things calm
You are the place to hide from harm
You are the light that shines in dark
You are the heart's eternal spark
You are the door that's open wide
You are the guest who waits inside
You are the stranger at the door
You are the calling of the poor
You are my Lord and with me still
You are my love, keep me from ill
You are the light, the truth, the way
You are my Savior this very day.

Morning Resolutions

SAMUEL JOHNSON

My purpose is from this time
To reject or expel sensual images, and idle thoughts.
To provide some useful amusement for leisure time.
To avoid idleness.
To rise early.
To study a proper portion of every day.
To worship God diligently.
To read the Scriptures.
To let no week pass without reading some part.
To write down my observations.
I will renew earlier resolutions.
I will not despair. I will pray to God
for resolution, and will endeavor to
strengthen my faith.

How Can I Keep From Singing?

ROBERT LOWRY

My life flows on in endless song;
Above earth's lamentation
I hear the sweet though far off hymn
That hails a new creation:
Through all the tumult and the strife
I hear the music ringing;
It finds an echo in my soul—
How can I keep from singing?

Be At Peace

ST. FRANCIS DE SALES

Do not look forward in fear
to the changes of life;

Rather look to them with full hope
that as they arise,

God, whose very own you are,
will lead you safely through all things;

And when you cannot stand it,
God will carry you in His arms.

Do not fear what may happen tomorrow;

The same everlasting Father
who cares for you today

will take care of you today and every day.

He will either shield you from suffering or
will give you unfailing strength to bear it.

Be at peace and put aside all
anxious thoughts and imaginations.

The Rhythm of Life

TRADITIONAL AFRICAN PRAYER

I am the drum,
You are the drum, and we are the drum.

Rhythm is the soul of life.
The whole universe revolves in rhythm.

Everything and every human action
revolve in rhythm.

The Way of
the Bodhisattva

A BUDDHIST MORNING PRAYER

For as long as space endures

And for as long as
living beings remain

Until then may I too abide

To dispel the misery of the world.

St. Patrick's Breastplate

ANCIENT CELTIC HYMN

I arise today through the strength
of the love of Cherubim

In obedience of Angels,
in the service of the Archangels,

In hope of resurrection
to meet with reward,

In prayers of Patriarchs,
in predictions of Prophets,

In preachings of Apostles,
in faiths of Confessors,

In innocence of Holy Virgins,
in deeds of righteous men.

I arise today, through the strength of Heaven;

Light of Sun, brilliance of Moon, splendor of Fire,

Speed of Lightning, swiftness of Wind, depth of Sea,

Stability of Earth, firmness of Rock.

I arise today, through God's strength to pilot me:

God's might to uphold me,

God's wisdom to guide me,

God's eye to look before me,

God's ear to hear me,

God's word to speak for me,

God's hand to guard me,

God's way to lie before me,

God's shield to protect me,

God's host to secure me:

Against snares of devils,

Against temptations of vices,

Against inclinations of nature,

Against everyone who shall wish me ill,

Afar and anear, alone and in a crowd.

Be Still

WILLIAM PENN

In the rush and noise of life,
as you have

Intervals, step within yourself
and be still.

Wait upon God and feel
his good presence;

This will carry you through
your day's business.

Prayers for Healing

In recovery, we learn that addiction is a disease that has damaged us physically, mentally, emotionally, and spiritually. Another word for recovery in this context would be healing. Once we cease living in active addiction we begin to get better and to repair the damage as best we can. In some areas, we bounce back quickly; others take longer, and some things may never be totally repaired. But, we do get better.

Healing is actually an extended conversation with God, a befriending of the flesh, mind, heart, and spirit that have been bruised and incised. Prayers of healing are especially important for us. We pray that our experiences of the pain and struggle of addiction be blessed with God's healing touch. We ask that God's grace and love wash over us and weave together the tattered strands of our hurting bodies, minds, emotions, and souls. We pray until our pain is eased into peace, and then we pray our thanks for the respite we have been granted.

The following prayers are a reminder to us that part of our healing process is to care for others with the same love and compassion we are given from others, and include two derived from Native American spirituality and a poem by John Donne. Some of the prayers focus on physical illness, others on spiritual malaise, still others make no distinction. The final prayer concerns HIV/AIDS, a disease to which we have lost many brethren in and out the rooms of recovery.

Lord, Please Help Me

AUTHOR UNKNOWN

Lord, please help me to bring
Comfort where there is pain
Courage where there is fear
Hope where there is despair
Acceptance when the end is near and
A touch of gentle with tenderness,
patience, and love.

She Who Heals

Mother, sing me a song
That will ease my pain,
Mend broken bones,
Bring wholeness again.

Catch my babies
When they are born,
Sing my death song,
Teach me how to mourn.

Show me the medicine
Of the healing arts,
The value of spirit,
The way I can serve.

Mother, heal my heart
So that I can see
The gifts of yours
That can live through me.

I Am Worthy
A Prayer for All Those in Recovery

REV. JOHN T. FARRELL

I am worthy of recovery, serenity, and a happy life.
I am worthy of achieving these things,
no matter what I have done up to this point in life
and whatever transgressions I may have committed.
I am still worthy.

I am competent and intelligent, no matter how badly
I did in school and what my employment history is.
I can make a contribution, no matter what anyone
has told me to the contrary. I alone have the means
to reach my dreams. I am worthy to live my dreams.

The road of life is difficult, not just for me,
but for everyone. It does me no good to compare
myself to others. All are worthy in the eyes of God
and all face unique challenges. I shall be honest
about who I am and will move away from my
preoccupation with self. It is not humility
to be something I am not or what others expect
me to be. I will be myself because I am worthy.

No one will give me my new life of recovery.
I am willing to work hard for it. I am willing
to accept the gifts and tools I have been given.
I am willing to transform myself into the good
and worthy person I was meant to be. I am
willing to pray and to serve others. I will
always remember that I am worthy.
And I will always be grateful.

As I Walk

TRADITIONAL NAVAJO PRAYER

As I walk, as I walk
The universe is walking with me
In beauty it walks before me
In beauty it walks behind me
In beauty it walks below me
In beauty it walks above me
Beauty is on every side
As I walk, I walk with Beauty.

The Prayer of John Donne

Bring us, O Lord God, at our last awakening
into the house and gate of Heaven,
to enter into that gate
and dwell in that house, where there shall be
no darkness nor dazzling, but one equal light;
no noise nor silence, but one equal music;
no fears or hopes, but one equal possession;
no ends or beginnings, but one equal eternity,
in the habitations of thy glory and dominion,
world without end. *Amen.*

A Prayer to Break Out of Complacency

CARYLL HOUSELANDER,
ATTRIBUTED, *SOUL WEAVINGS*

We are the mediocre,
we are the half-givers,
we are the half-lovers,
we are the savourless salt.

Break the hard crust
of complacency.
Quicken in us
the sharp grace of desire.

A Prayer of Hope

It is not what I am
nor what I have been that
God sees with his all-merciful eyes,
but what I desire to be.

From *Cloud of Unknowing*

A Prayer for the Suffering Addict

REV. JOHN T. FARRELL

Essence of Love, bestow your spirit
on those addicts who are in despair.
Comfort them, in their time of pain,
and relieve them of their isolation.
Cast away from them the specter of
despair and destruction that enfolds them.
Help them that they may be free from
the shackles of addiction. Let them
come to know that life is precious and
recovery is a gift to be nurtured.
Remember and help all addicts who suffer,
in and out of the rooms of recovery,
and keep them in your heart.

For the Addicted

O great Physician, who through your
humanity entered into the sufferings of the sick,
fill with your healing gifts all who are
in any way addicted. Grant them your strength,
your forgiveness, and your sustaining love.
Of your mercy release them and restore them,
that they may know the joy of life in your service.

From *Prayers New and Old* (2007 Edition)

Copyright © 2009–2010. Used by permission of Forward Movement
Publications, Cincinnati, Ohio.

A Prayer for Healing for People with HIV/AIDS

REV. JOHN T. FARRELL

Source of Love and Healing, many
of my brothers and sisters live with
HIV and AIDS. I believe you have given
our fellowship the mission to restore addicts
to recovery and healing. Guide us as we
help those among us who are broken
in spirit and body by HIV/AIDS. May the
fellowship they find in recovery overcome
their marginalization. May the reconciliation
of the Twelve Steps heal their guilt and help
their spirits find freedom from active addiction.
May their recovery triumph over their
despair and may our understanding conquer
their estrangement. *Amen.*

Prayers for Acceptance

Acceptance at so many levels can be difficult for those in recovery. Our first difficulty is often accepting ourselves and accepting that God and others love us. That's why I selected the seventeenth-century writer George Herbert's poem "Love" to begin this chapter. In it, Herbert describes a person who is frightened to accept God's open-hearted love. The person desires love, but feels the weakness of mortality and the weight of human defects that are universal to humanity. But love knows the secrets of our hearts and accepts us as we are. So God persuades the person to sit down at the table for a feast. Other prayers in this chapter address our ongoing need to continue to accept our limitations, those of others, and the circumstances of our lives. These prayers also express the hope we all have that we grow and improve and that things will get better a day at a time.

Other prayers in this chapter come from medieval to modern sources. The medieval is represented by Lady Julian of Norwich, a thirteenth century mystic whose optimistic belief in a loving God still inspires. The most modern are prayers about "letting go" and accountability, two themes intrinsic to spiritual recovery.

Love

GEORGE HERBERT

Love bade me welcome, yet my soul drew back,
Guilty of dust and sin.
But quick-ey'd Love, observing me grow slack
From my first entrance in,
Drew nearer to me, sweetly questioning
If I lack'd anything.

"A guest," I answer'd, "worthy to be here,"
Love said, "You shall be he."
"I, the unkind, the ungrateful? ah my dear,
I cannot look on thee."
Love took my hand and smiling did reply,
"Who made the eyes but I?"

"Truth, Lord, but I have marr'd them; let my shame
Go where it doth deserve."
"And know you not," says Love,
"who bore the blame?"
"My dear, then I will serve."
"You must sit down," says Love,
"and taste my meat."
So I did sit and eat.

Prayer of Acceptance

REV. JOHN T. FARRELL

Source of my strength,
never allow me to become victim to
self-pity and despair. Help me realize that
life's futility begins and ends in waves
of piteous self-indulgence. Help me avoid
self-pity and despair. Let me accept life
on life's terms, not mine. *Amen.*

Prayer for Patience and Gentleness

JOHANN ARNDT

Bestow on me, O Lord,
a genial spirit and
unwearied forbearance;
a mild, loving, patient, heart;
kindly looks, pleasant
cordial speech, and manners
in the exchanges of daily life;
that I may give offence to none,
but as much as in lies,
live in charity with all.

Three Prayerful Questions Times Two

REV. JOHN T. FARRELL

What have I done
for my recovery?

What am I doing
for my recovery?

What should I be doing
for my recovery?

What have I done
for another addict's recovery?

What am I doing
for another addict's recovery?

What should I be doing
for another addict's recovery?

Prayer for Generosity

ST. IGNATIUS OF LOYOLA

Teach me true generosity.

Teach me to serve you as you deserve.

To give without counting the cost,

To fight heedless of wounds,

To labor without seeking rest,

To sacrifice myself without
thought of any reward,

Save the knowledge that
I have done your will. *Amen.*

Prayer of Acceptance

LADY JULIAN OF NORWICH

God did not say,
"You shall not be tempest-tossed;
you shall not be work-weary;
you shall not be discomforted."
But God did say,
"You shall not be overcome."
God wants us to heed these words
so that we shall always be strong in trust,
both in sorrow and in joy. *Amen.*

To Let Go

ANONYMOUS

To "let go" does not mean to stop caring;
It means I can't do it for someone else.

To "let go" is not to cut myself off;
It is the realization that
I must not control another.

To "let go" is not to fix;
But to be supportive.

To "let go" is not to be in the middle
Arranging all the outcomes;
But to allow others to effect their destinies.

To "let go" is not to be protective;
It is to permit another to face reality.
To "let go" is not to regret the past;
But to grow and live for the future.

To "let go" is to fear less
And love more.

A Prayer for Forgiveness

QUR'AN 23:109

Our Lord! We believe,
therefore forgive us
and have mercy on us
for Thou art best
of all who show mercy.

A Prayer for Accountability

REV. JOHN T. FARRELL

Ground of my being, relieve me of my
defensiveness and perfectionism. May I
stop making excuses for my behavior and
become honest about myself. May I stop
blaming others for my setbacks and look inside
myself. May I avoid victimhood and take
responsibility for who I am and what I do.
May I own up to my shortcomings
and accept accountability. May I remember
always that I am loved for who I am now,
not for an image of who I should be or
of who I want to be. Let me accept myself
for all my weaknesses and strengths
and with all my flaws and virtues. *Amen.*

Third Step Prayers

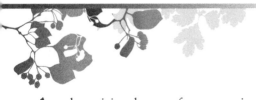

At the spiritual core of recovery is the Third Step. This step explicitly mentions the role of God in our recovery by asking us to turn our lives and our will over to God's care. It honors our independence of thought and choice by allowing us to define God in terms of our own understanding, spiritual needs, and background. The rewards of taking the Third Step are immediately apparent even to those in early recovery. In 1939, with only four years of abstinence, Bill Wilson (co-founder of Alcoholics Anonymous) was able to describe the Third Step in these eloquent terms, ". . .As we felt new power flow in, as we enjoyed peace of mind, as we discovered we could face life successfully, as we became conscious of His presence, we began to lose our fear of today, tomorrow, or the hereafter. We were reborn."*

* Alcoholics Anonymous, p. 63

Similarly, thirty years later, the authors of *Narcotics Anonymous* (the recovery text for the Narcotics Anonymous fellowship) wrote ". . .Our fears are lessened and faith begins to grow as we learn the true meaning of surrender. We are no longer fighting fear, anger, guilt, self-pity, or depression. We realize that what brought us to this program is still with us today and will continue to guide us if we allow it. We are slowly beginning to lose the paralyzing fear of hopelessness. The proof of this step is in the way we live."*

The prayers in this chapter offer a multiplicity of ways to form a relationship with God through prayer and the Third Step. This chapter contains Third Step prayers from various twelve-step fellowships and several other prayers that many people in recovery find useful, most notably the Serenity Prayer and the Prayer of St. Francis. The point is that there is no specific prayer that *must* be used; just a simple prayer to confirm our willingness to take action as a result of our decision to turn our will over to the care of God. We need merely to pray with as much as we understand of ourselves to as much as we understand of a God.

---

* Reprinted by permission of NA World Services, Inc. All rights reserved.

Third Step Prayer

NARCOTICS ANONYMOUS

Take my will and my life.

Guide me in my recovery.

Show me how to live.

Reprinted by permission of NA World
Services, Inc. All rights reserved.

Third Step Prayer

ALCOHOLICS ANONYMOUS

God, I offer myself to Thee—to build
with me and to do with me as Thou wilt.
Relieve me of the bondage of self, that I may
better do Thy will. Take away my difficulties,
that victory over them may bear witness
to those I would help of Thy Power,
Thy Love, and Thy Way of life.

May I do Thy will always.

Alternative Third Step Prayer in Contemporary English

REV. JOHN T. FARRELL

I give myself to God to be used as God wishes.
May I be relieved of the bondage of self,
so I may better do God's will. May my fears,
my selfishness, and self-centeredness be taken
away so I can be an example to others
of God's power, love, and way of life.
May I do God's will always.

Third Step Prayer

CODEPENDENTS ANONYMOUS

God, I give to You all that I am and all that
I will be for Your healing and direction.
Make new this day as I release all my worries
and fears, knowing that You are by my side.
Please help me to open myself to Your love,
to allow Your love to heal my wounds,
and to allow Your love to flow through me
and from me to those around me.
May Your will be done
this day and always. *Amen.*

Reprinted by permission of Codependents Anonymous.
All rights reserved.

Jewish Third Step Prayer

REB NOSSON

Grant me inner peace. . .
Let my body be completely subordinate
to my soul and have no other will or desire
but to follow the desire of the holy soul,
which is to do Your will.

Let peace reign between my soul and my body.
Let my body be sanctified and purified
until it becomes united with the holy soul
and I carry out all Your commandments
and do everything You want of me,
body and soul, willingly and with great joy.

Let my body and soul unite in love and peace
to do Your will sincerely, until I attain
complete inner harmony and am ready
to order my prayer before You perfectly.

Let my prayer rise before You like
the incense and perfect sacrifices offered
by those who are whole and perfect.

NA Third Step Prayer

God, I am now willing to put my life
in your care. Align my will with Yours and
help me to recognize and carry out your will.

Open my heart so I may be a free
and open channel for your love.

Take away my fears and doubts,
that I may better demonstrate
Your presence in my life.

May your will, not mine, be done.

From an unpublished draft of
It Works: How and Why

Reprinted by permission of NA World
Services, Inc. All rights reserved.

The Third Step Is Tougher Than I Thought

REV. JOHN T. FARRELL

Hey God, I know that I can't do this
recovery thing all by myself. So, I go to meetings,
call my sponsor, and drink endless cups of coffee.
And talk, talk endlessly about myself.
But sometimes I even remember to listen.
So, why do I sometimes forget to talk to you?
Weren't you on my list of things to do?

Here's my prayer then: give me the willingness
to keep you at the top of my list and to
keep my priorities clear—you, recovery, family,
friends, community, career. Help me remember
that you are the top of the list. Remind me
that I have decided to turn my will and my life
over to you. Only you can give me the help
that I need for a lasting recovery.

Native American
Third Step Prayer

Great Spirit,

Whose voice I hear in the wind,

Whose breath gives life
to the world,

Hear me.

I come to you as one of
your many children,

I am small and weak,

I need your strength and wisdom.

May I walk in beauty.

And how my life
is unmanageable.

I need to learn
and remember that

I have an incurable illness and that

Abstinence is the only way
to deal with it.

With Every Breath

BUDDHIST THIRD STEP PRAYER

With every breath I take today,
I vow to be awake;

And every step I take,
I vow to take with a grateful heart—

So I may see with eyes of love
Into the hearts of all I meet,

To ease their burden when I can
And touch them with a smile of peace.

I take refuge in the Buddha,
Dharma, and Sangha
Until I attain Enlightenment.
By merit accumulations from practicing
generosity and the other perfections
May I attain Enlightenment,
for the benefit of all sentient beings.

Third Step Prayer

(*Both sponsor and protégé/sponsee on their knees*)

Sponsor says: God, this is _____; he (she)
is coming to You in all humility to ask You to
guide and direct him (her). _____ realizes
that his (her) life is messed up and unmanageable.
_____ is coming to You Lord in all humility
to ask to be one of your children—to work for you,
to serve and dedicate his (her) life to you,
and to turn his (her) will over that he (she)
may be an instrument of your love.

(*Protégé/sponsee repeats after the sponsor*)

Lord, I ask that you guide and direct me,
and that I have decided to turn my life and
will over to you. To serve You and to dedicate
my life to You. I thank you Lord, I believe that
if I ask this in prayer, I shall receive what
I have asked for. Thank you God. *Amen.*

Attributed to the members of
the first AA group in Cleveland

Third Step Prayer

AUTHOR UNKNOWN

Thank you for taking my resentments,
fears, and negative emotions. Please give me
the power to continue the action of giving them
to you, so I may continue the action of doing
my best at doing your will. Thank you for letting
me trust you, for I know now that I cannot
handle everything and everybody by myself.
Please help me recognize when I'm being selfish
and self-seeking, so I may use that energy to be
selfless and help consider others' feelings and
actions. Please continue all my positive actions,
and I promise to take it day by day.
Thanks again God!

Prayer of St. Francis

ST. FRANCIS OF ASSISI

O Lord, make me an instrument of Thy Peace!
Where there is hatred, let me sow love.
Where there is injury, pardon.
Where there is discord, harmony.
Where there is doubt, faith.
Where there is despair, hope.
Where there is darkness, light.
Where there is sorrow, joy.

Oh Divine Master, grant that I may not
so much seek to be consoled as to console;
to be understood as to understand;
to be loved as to love;
for it is in giving that we receive;
it is in pardoning that we are pardoned;
and it is in dying that we are
born to Eternal Life.

Psalm 103:1–8

THE BOOK OF COMMON PRAYER

1. Bless the Lord, O my soul, and all
that is within me, bless his holy Name.

2. Bless the Lord, O my soul,
and forget not all his benefits.

3. He forgives all your sins
and heals all your infirmities;

4. He redeems your life from the grave and
crowns you with mercy and loving-kindness;

5. He satisfies you with good things,
and your youth is renewed like an eagle's.

6. The Lord executes righteousness
and judgment for all who are oppressed.

7. He made his ways known to Moses
and his works to the children of Israel.

8. The Lord is full of compassion and mercy,
slow to anger and of great kindness.

The Serenity Prayer
Original Version

REINHOLD NIEBUHR

God, grant me the serenity
to accept the things I cannot change,
the courage to change the things I can,
and the wisdom to know the difference.

The Serenity Prayer
Enhanced Version

DANIEL KAELIN

God, give me the serenity to accept
that which I cannot change, strength to
change that which I can, and the insight to
know the difference; living only for today,
for this hour, for this moment; accepting life's
challenges as a way to find peace; accepting
those who live in sin, and trusting that if I
surrender my will that you will allow me
to be truly happy in this life and to serve you
in my future in this life and in the next life
when I join you in your kingdom. *Amen.*

Serenity Prayer
Humorous Version

God grant me the serenity
to accept the people I cannot change,

Courage to change
the one I can change,

And wisdom to know it's me.

Prayers for the Ups and Downs of Life

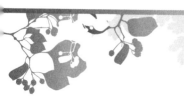

"Life is difficult," says author Scott Peck in his book, *The Road Less Traveled*. Many people living in active addiction would agree with that statement and then proceed to use life's difficulties as a reason to continue in their self-destruction. In reality, addicts can use anything as a reason to continue living in active addiction, whether it is difficulty, cause for celebration, sheer boredom, or addressing the myriad of daily life experiences because they are afraid to experience life. But difficulty is not the whole of life. Life is also filled with joy, mystery, challenge, humiliation, victory, lessons, ignobility, and triumphs.

In recovery, however, we learn to cope with all of life in its messiness, reversal, and unexpectedness. Recovery teaches us to live life on life's terms, not on our terms, and certainly not on the terms set by the disease of addiction. If we remain connected to God, other recovering addicts, and the program, we can face anything and do anything.

The following prayers address some of the daily life situations that addicts in recovery might face. It is hardly exhaustive. Many of the prayers can be adapted and reworked for particular situations. The prayers address some of the challenges of modern life such as unemployment, financial instability, test taking, depression, and anger. It includes a list of arrow prayers, that is, short prayers that one can fly to heaven at any time and any place. The phrase "arrow prayer" was coined by Augustine of Hippo to describe a manner of prayer that lends itself to a rhythmic repetition that facilitates meditation and inner stillness. The best ones are just a few words in length like, "God help me!"

Prayer for Success

REV. JOHN T. FARRELL

This day was created for gain not loss,
success not failure.

This day was created for
positive actions not negative thoughts.

May I use the gifts and talents that have so
generously been given to me in my recovery.

They are tools to be used,
not treasures to be stored up. *Amen.*

Prayer for When I Fail

REV. JOHN T. FARRELL

God of mercy, you know the secrets of my heart;
you know the pureness of my motives and
my desire to do well. Hear my prayer in the
midst of my latest failure; give me patience,
humility, and hope, so that under your protection
and with you as my guide, I will live for another
day to serve your will and straighten the
path of my life. *Amen.*

Prayer for
Financial Healing

REV. JOHN T. FARRELL

Source of abundance, my life is shattered
by poor decisions and broken finances. Please
help me find a measure of financial security
in my chaotic life. Grant me the ability to pay
my bills, to maintain shelter, and to obtain daily
bread for myself and those in my care. Help
me to provide for my health needs and those
of my family. Give me strength, courage,
and optimism in the midst of my financial
uncertainty. Let me be creative, resourceful,
and, above all, hopeful as I seek financial
healing. Let me address any personal
accountability in my finances and let
me accept economic forces that are
beyond my control. *Amen.*

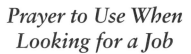

Prayer to Use When Looking for a Job

REV. VICTOR FUHRMAN

Heavenly Father, please sustain my spirit as
I search for new and meaningful work.
You have blessed me with a healthy body and
a keen mind for which I am grateful. I ask that
you open my path as I seek employment that
will allow me to support my family and myself
while serving others and your divine purpose.
In gratitude and grace. *Amen.*

Copyright ©2010. Reverend Victor Fuhrman.
Used with permission.

Prayer for a Sense of Humor

REV. JOHN T. FARRELL

Thank you God for the gift of laughter,
for blessing humanity with humor and
for giving me an abundance of things to
laugh about. May I always see the funny side
of life, especially in the things that happen
to me and in the situations I may find myself.
Let me use humor, not as a weapon, but as
a tool to relieve tension, to bring about
reconciliation, to connect with others,
and to cement relationships. In times of
adversity, allow me to find something to
laugh about so I do not succumb to ill-temper,
anger, and despair. Let me greet the world
with a smile as I go about my daily life.

Prayer for the Stressful Day

JOHN HENRY NEWMAN

May He support us all the day long,

till the shades lengthen,
and the evening comes,

and the busy world is hushed,

and the fever of life is over
and our work is done!

Then in His mercy may
He give us a safe lodging,

and a holy rest, and peace at the last.

Prayer Before a Test

REV. JOHN T. FARRELL

Source of Knowledge, studying is so stressful
for me and tests give me so much anxiety.
Right now, a test looms large and it is all
I can think about. Give me confidence in my
ability to master the material. Give me the
courage to overcome my fear of failure.
Give me the maturity to enjoy learning for
learning's sake. Help me to do my best,
be satisfied with the result, and to put this
test and all tests in the perspective of
a life committed to intellectual growth
and increase of knowledge. *Amen.*

Listening

MARY L. KUPFERLE

I take time to be quiet, to be still and
contemplate the Truth that God's love is
right there with me; that God's light is now
shining throughout my mind to reveal what
I need to see and know. I listen within and
let God's wisdom gently turn my thoughts
over and over until the questions become
answers, the doubts become newborn faith.
I will see that everything has been and
is working for my good.

Adapted from *God Will See You Through*

A Prayer for
Loss of Temper

REV. JOHN T. FARRELL

Sometimes my anger controls my behavior
and I cannot help myself. I want to be calm
and cool, but cannot. I must overcome these
rampant emotions and negative hostility
or I will damage myself and others.
Help me, God, help me. Pour your gentleness
over my troubled spirit. Heal me of my
quick temper and loss of self-control.
Grant me serenity and help me grow
into the gentleness and maturity that I seek
as part of my recovering life. *Amen.*

A Prayer for Divine Companionship

MARIA W. STEWART

O Lord God, as the heavens are high above the earth, so are Thy ways above our ways, and Thy thoughts above our thoughts. For wise and holy purposes best known to Thyself, Thou hast seen fit to deprive me of all earthly relatives; but when my father and mother forsook me, then Thou did take me up. I desire to thank Thee, that I am this day a living witness to testify that Thou art a God that will ever vindicate the cause of the poor and needy, and that Thou hast always proved Thyself to be a friend and father to me. O, continue Thy loving kindness even unto the end; and when health and strength begin to decay, and I, as it were, draw nigh unto the grave, O then afford me Thy heart-cheering presence, and enable me to rely entirely upon Thee. Never leave me nor forsake me, but have mercy upon me for Thy great name's sake. And not for myself alone do I ask these blessings, but for all the poor and needy, all widows and fatherless children, for the stranger in distress; and may they call upon Thee in such manner as to be convinced that Thou art a prayer-hearing and prayer-answering God; and thine shall be the praise, forever. *Amen.*

Let Go and Let God
Arrow Prayers from the Daily Word

✣ God is the source of limitless good that
is continually blessing me.

✣ I am flexible as I allow God's plan
to emerge and evolve.

✣ I let go and let my faith
in God carry me through.

✣ With a silent, heartfelt prayer,
I let go and let God
heal my relationships.

✣ I let go and let God,
knowing that the source
of all good is in charge.

Affirmations from *Daily Word* magazine.
Reprinted with permission of Unity,
publisher of *Daily Word*.

Prayer for a Recovering Addict Who Is Depressed

REV. JOHN T. FARRELL

Today I am walking through a vale of
despair and depression. I am unloved and unlovely,
rejected and despised, of no use to myself and
others, alienated and isolated. I am lost
in a world in which I have no place. Sometimes
I want to go to sleep and just not wake up.

I know this is not the way I am meant to feel.
Yet, even though I believe in the transforming
power of love and the miracle of recovery, I still
suffer from these dismal and destructive thoughts.

Spirit of Love, I cry out to you. Enfold me in your
arms and give me comfort. Ease my mind and
soothe my turmoil. I am in a desert and want to find
an oasis. I am broken and want to be whole. I am
disconnected and want to be *a part of*, not *apart
from*. I am an island and want to join the mainland.

Heal me. Make me whole. Let me feel the joy and
passion of life. Let me find the help and succor I need.

Prayer for Protection

EPHESIANS 6: 13-17

Therefore put on the full armor of God,
so that when the day of evil comes,
you may be able to stand your ground,
and after you have done everything, to stand.
Stand firm then, with the belt of truth buckled
around your waist, with the breastplate of
righteousness in place, and with your feet
fitted with the readiness that comes from
the gospel of peace. In addition to all this,
take up the shield of faith, with which you can
extinguish all the flaming arrows of the evil one.
Take the helmet of salvation and the sword
of the Spirit, which is the word of God.

Prayers for Relationships

Relationships seem to cause more joy and more anguish than anything else in our recovery. During our active addiction, we were isolated and alienated from so much and so many, and when we finally came into recovery, we longed to rectify our loneliness, isolation, and alienation. As human beings, we yearn for the comfort and solace of a partner to love and support us in our mutual life. Life, of course, is made up of relationships—with God, with ourselves, and with other people. As so eloquently suggested in the Twelve Steps, before we can have a successful one-on-one relationship with another person, we need to establish a pattern of right relationships with God and ourselves. Then we will be ready for the joy and challenges of a long-term, committed, and unconditional love.

Prayer is integral to a good relationship. The prayers and poems in this chapter focus on our ability to love and our desire to devote our being to one person. Some mention marriage, but all are predicated on the belief that most of us are called to a state of bonding and coupling with another human being in love and harmony. These thoughtful reflections offer guidance to help us achieve this.

A Prayer of the Claddagh

REV. JOHN T. FARRELL

In Celtic spirituality, the combination of heart,
hands, and crown is known as the Claddagh,
a visual portrayal of the eternal bond
of friendship, loyalty, and love.

In the spirit of the Claddagh, I pray that:

My heart will symbolize love, life's finest impulse.
From my heart, may generosity and compassion flow.

My hands will be clasped around my heart
in a gesture of connection. As they cradle my
heart gently, may my hands be protective
and strong, like true friendship.

The crown will represent loyalty as the
reward of love, the highest achievement
the human spirit has yet accomplished.

To live by the Claddagh is to forge forever
the bonds of love, connection, and loyalty
in my relationships.

Metta Karuna Prayer

G. R. LEWIS

Oneness of Life and Light,

Entrusting in your
Great Compassion,

May you shed the
foolishness in myself,

Transforming me
into a conduit of Love.

Prayer for a Couple

Give us wisdom and devotion in the ordering
of our common life, that each may be to the other
a strength in need, a counselor in perplexity,
a comfort in sorrow, and a companion in joy.

Grant that our wills may be so knit together
in your will, and our spirits in your Spirit,
that we may grow in love and peace with you
and one another all the days of our life.

Give us grace, when we hurt each other,
to recognize and acknowledge our fault,
and to seek each other's forgiveness and yours.

Make our life together a sign of love to this
sinful and broken world, that unity may
overcome estrangement, forgiveness heal guilt,
and joy conquer despair.

Give us such fulfillment of our mutual
affection that we may reach out in
love and concern for others. *Amen.*

Adapted from *The Book of Common Prayer*

Ten Ways to Destroy a Relationship

REV. JOHN T. FARRELL

Dear God, if I ever decide to destroy a relationship,
please help me with the following:

Making everything in life about me.

Making little things bother me.
Not just letting them, making them.

Being anxious about everything.

Finding fault frequently.

Being right. Being always right.
Being the only one who is always right.

Being jealous and mistrustful.

Being suspicious and insisting
that others have hidden motives.

Being entitled.

Taking everything personally.

Never committing fully to anything.

A Prayer for Growing Older

ANONYMOUS

Keep me from thinking that I must
express myself on every subject and straighten
out everyone's affairs. Keep me from the recital
of endless detail and give me wings to get to the
point. Seal my lips on my aches and pains,
for the love of rehearsing them becomes sweeter
as the years go by. And when I grow weary of
hearing of the aches and pains of others, may
I endure their recitation patiently. Make me
thoughtful but not moody, helpful but not bossy,
concerned but not nosey. Give me eyes to see beauty
in unexpected places and talents in unexpected
people, and give me the grace to tell them so.
I dare not ask for improved memory, but for a
growing humility when others' memories differ
from mine. Teach me that occasionally I may
be mistaken. With my vast store of wisdom,
it seems a pity not to dispense it all, but you know,
Lord, that I want a few friends at the end.

A Prayer to Preserve a Relationship

REV. JOHN T. FARRELL

Let us remember our beginning, when
our optimism was great and the love between
us was vibrant. May we keep those memories
fresh so we can weather the storms that
inevitably will come. Let our relationship
not grow stale and let us not take each
other for granted. We pledge that our
words will always be kind and loving
and our hearts always forgiving
and contrite. *Amen.*

A Marriage Blessing

AUTHOR UNKNOWN

We thank You, O God, for the love
You have implanted in our hearts. May it
always inspire us to be kind in our words,
considerate of feelings, and concerned
for each other's needs and wishes. Help us
to be understanding and forgiving of human
weaknesses and failings. Increase our faith
and trust in You and may Your prudence
guide our life and love. Bless our marriage,
O God, with peace and happiness,
and make our love fruitful for Your glory
and our joy both here and in eternity.

What Greater Thing

GEORGE ELIOT

What greater thing is there for two human souls,
than to feel that they are joined for life—
to strengthen each other in all labor,
to rest on each other in all sorrow,
to minister to each other in all pain,
to be one with each other
in silent unspeakable memories.

Love Is Patient

1 CORINTHIANS 13:4-8, 13 (NIV)

Love is patient, love is kind.
It does not envy, it does not boast,
it is not proud. It is not rude,
it is not self-seeking,
it is not easily angered,
it keeps no record of wrongs.

Love does not delight in evil
but rejoices with the truth.
It always protects, always trusts,
always hopes, always perseveres.
Love never fails. . . .

And now these three remain:
faith, hope, and love.

But the greatest of these is love.

When Two People Are at One

When two people are at one
in their inmost hearts
They shatter even the strength of iron
or of bronze
And when two people understand each other
in their inmost hearts
Their words are sweet and strong
like the fragrance of orchids.

From the *I Ching*

A German Blessing

With faith there is love,
With love there is peace,
With peace there is blessing,
With blessing there is God,
With God there is no need.

The Madness of Love

HADEWIJCH OF ANTWERP

The madness of love
Is a blessed fate;
And if we understand this
We would seek no other:
It brings into unity
What was divided,
And this is the truth:
Bitterness it makes sweet,
It makes the stranger
a neighbor,
And what was lowly
it raises on high.

On Marriage

KAHLIL GIBRAN

You were born together, and
together you shall be forevermore.

You shall be together when the
white wings of death scatter your days.

Aye, you shall be together
even in the silent memory of God.

But let there be spaces in your togetherness,

And let the winds of the heavens
dance between you.

Love one another,
but make not a bond of love:

Let it rather be a moving sea
between the shores of your souls.

Fill each other's cup but
drink not from one cup.

Give one another of your bread
but eat not from the same loaf.

Sing and dance together and be joyous,
but let each one of you be alone,

Even as the strings of a lute are alone
though they quiver with the same music.

Give your hearts,
but not into each other's keeping.

For only the hand of Life
can contain your hearts.

And stand together
yet not too near together:

For the pillars of the temple stand apart,

And the oak tree and the cypress
grow not in each other's shadow.

Psalm 102
When I Am Lonely

A prayer of one afflicted, when
faint and pleading before the Lord.

1. Hear my prayer, O Lord;
   let my cry come to you.

2. Do not hide your face from me
   on the day of my distress.

3. Incline your ear to me; answer me
   speedily on the day when I call.

Prayers for Protection

A Zen master once claimed that most people live in two minds, fear and joy. He may be right, but we often find ourselves living in fear, even after getting into recovery. We are plagued by vague anxieties, unreasonable apprehensions, and bouts of terror. Our fears are manifested as we live in our regret of the past or in our worry over the future. In recovery, we learn that living in fear is part of the *dis*-ease of the disease of addiction. Living a day at a time is the greatest antidote to fear because joy is discovered by living in the present—when we shed the past, let go of the future, and are just there, where we are, in that moment. We learn then that we are protected, protected by a power of goodness greater than ourselves that will keep us in safety.

One way to invoke God's protection and blessing is through prayer. In this chapter, there are a variety of prayers for seeking protection and safety. Many of them are ancient, since the need for protection is great in all cultures. One is from the Hindu tradition, another from Native American spirituality, still another from Kenya. There are two versions of Psalm 23, the classic version and a second written especially for people in recovery. The one by John Henry Newman is phrased in stately Victorian language, followed by the simple words of St. Patrick translated from Latin. All ask for the same thing: protection from the perils of the world, both from without and within.

Big Sea, Little Boat
ANCIENT FISHERMAN'S PRAYER

Dear God, be good to me;
The sea is so wide,
And my boat is so small.
Amen.

Hindu Prayer for Protection

Day by day does man
come nearer to death;

His youth wears away;
the day that is gone never returns.

Almighty Time devours everything;

Fickle as lightning is the
goddess of fortune.

O Siva! O Giver of shelter to
those that come to Thee for refuge!

Protect me, who have
taken refuge at Thy feet.

From the *Gospel of Sri Ramakrishna*

From Sri Shankaracharya's Hymn to Siva for Forgiveness
as quoted from page 1002 of the *Gospel of Sri Ramakrishna*
by Swami Nikhilananda (translator), copyright 1942.
Published by the Ramakrishna-Vivekananda
Center of New York.

Prayer for Peace

HAZRAT INAYAT KHAN

Send Thy peace O Lord, which is perfect and
everlasting, that our souls may radiate peace.

Send Thy peace O Lord, that we may
think, act, and speak harmoniously.

Send Thy peace O Lord, that we may be
contented and thankful for Thy bountiful gifts.

Send Thy peace O Lord, that amidst our
worldly strife, we may enjoy Thy bliss.

Send Thy peace O Lord, that we may endure all,
tolerate all, in the thought of Thy grace and mercy.

Send Thy peace O Lord, that our
lives may become a Divine vision and
in Thy light, all darkness may vanish.

Send Thy peace O Lord, our Father and Mother,
that we Thy children on Earth may
all unite in one family. *Amen.*

A Prayer of Faith

JAMES 5:10–16

Are any among you suffering?
They should pray. Are any cheerful?
They should sing songs of praise. Are any
among you sick? They should call for the elders
and have them pray over them, anointing
them with oil in the name of the Lord. The prayer
of faith will save the sick, and the Lord will raise
them up; and anyone who has committed sins
will be forgiven. Therefore confess your sins
to one another, and pray for one another,
so that you may be healed. The prayer of the
righteous is powerful and effective.

Prayer to Grandfather Great Spirit

SIOUX PRAYER

All over the world the faces
of living ones are alike.
With tenderness they have
come up out of the ground.
Look upon your children
that they may face the winds
and walk the good road to the Day of Quiet.
Grandfather Great Spirit
fill us with the Light.
Give us the strength to understand,
and the eyes to see.
Teach us to walk the soft Earth
as relatives to all that live.

Psalm 23
Classic Version

HOLY BIBLE
KING JAMES VERSION

The Lord is my shepherd; I shall not want.

He maketh me to lie down in green pastures:

He leadeth me beside the still waters.

He restoreth my soul:

He leadeth me in the paths of
righteousness for His name's sake.

Yea, though I walk through the valley
of the shadow of death,

I will fear no evil: for Thou art with me;

Thy rod and thy staff comfort me.

Thou preparest a table before me
in the presence of mine enemies:

Thou anointest my head with oil;

My cup runneth over.

Surely goodness and mercy shall
follow me all the days of my life:

And I will dwell in the
house of the Lord forever.

Psalm 23
For Those in Recovery

REV. JOHN T. FARRELL

God is my sponsor, and I shall not want.

God gives me the peace of the steps, so I can find repose in still waters amid the turbulence.

God inspires me to pray before I speak and encourages me to live life on life's terms.

God is the Power greater than myself, not my ego.

God restores my sanity a day at a time and guides my decisions that I might grow in love.

Though I may endure the compulsion to return to my addiction, I will not, for God is with me!

God's presence, God's peace, and God's power will get me through anything.

God raises me up, even when I am despondent, depressed, and despairing.

And, at the end of the day, God will be there to meet me so I can experience joy forever.

Kenyan Prayer

From the cowardice that dare not
Face new truth,
From the laziness that is contented
With half truth,
From the arrogance that thinks it
Knows all truth,
Good Lord, deliver me.

Prayer for God's Protection

Almighty and merciful God,
in your goodness keep us, we pray,
from all things that may hurt us, that we,
being ready both in mind and body,
may accomplish with free hearts
what belongs to Your purpose.

From *Prayers New and Old* (2007 Edition)

Copyright © 2009–2010. Used by permission of
Forward Movement Publications, Cincinnati, Ohio.

Lead Kindly Light

JOHN HENRY NEWMAN

Lead kindly Light, amid the
encircling gloom, lead Thou me on!

The night is dark, and I am far
from home, lead Thou me on!

Keep Thou my feet! I do not ask to see

The distant scene; one step enough for me.

I was not ever thus, nor prayed
that Thou shouldst lead me on:

I loved to choose and see my path;
but now lead Thou me on!

I loved the garish day, and, spite of fears,

Pride ruled my will—remember not past years!

So long Thy power hath blest me,
sure it still will lead me on.

O'er moor and fen, o'er crag and torrent,
till the night is gone,

And with the morn those
angel faces smile, which I

Have loved long since, and lost awhile.

The Light of God

The Light of God before me.
The Light of God behind me.
The Light of God above me.
The Light of God beside me.
The Light of God within me.

From *Prayer of St. Patrick*

The Three Jewels

I take refuge in the Buddha,
Dharma, and Sangha

Until I attain Enlightenment.

By merit accumulations from
practicing generosity
and the other perfections

May I attain Enlightenment,
for the benefit of all sentient beings.

Prayers for Walking through the Shadows

In our active addiction, we often feel at war with a world that looks upon us with contempt and misunderstands the nature of our disease. Each day we stand firm as we defend our self-destruction. At the root of our defensive posture are the demons of fear, mistrust, and a sense of entitlement. Even deeper than those negative emotions is our own self-loathing and the fear that people might be as awful as we think we are. These thoughts, along with our awareness of our usual human frailties, might be best termed our shadows.

In recovery, we learn to live in the light by first learning to get along with ourselves. As we come to realize that God and others love us just as we are, we learn to walk out of the shadows and love ourselves for who we are. Once that happens, most of our so-called "enemies" disappear, and we learn to either accept them as they are or to become friends with them. We appreciate the wisdom of Mahatma Ghandi's observation that it is easy enough to be gracious to friends, but to be friendly with our enemies is the mark of true religion.

The prayers in this chapter are representative of the universal desire to be at peace with ourselves and with our neighbors. Some address the struggles we all face in our efforts to maintain self-control while others reflect the quest for peace and serenity. There is one grouping that gives a number of variations of the Golden Rule throughout different traditions. These make excellent arrow prayers. Of special interest are the Beatitudes written by Mildred Norman Ryder, a spiritual teacher and peace prophet, who was known to many by the pseudonym, Peace Pilgrim.

Prayer to Overcome Aggression

REV. JOHN T. FARRELL

Aggressiveness is not truly my nature.

Aggressiveness, touchiness, and
defensiveness are symptoms of addiction.

Being pushy, demanding, and threatening are
the ways an addict controls and dominates.

May I learn patience and gentleness to persuade
others and to accept disagreement.

May I learn to employ assertiveness
in a peaceful manner when needed.

For it is obligatory to speak up when
a wrong has been implemented.

I trust in Your wisdom to guide me! *Amen.*

From the Qur'an

AL-FURQUAN, PART 19, CHAPTER 25

The true servants of the Gracious GOD
are the following: Those who walk upon
earth with humility and when they are tempted
by the evil ones, they respond: Peace; Those
who pass the hours of the night in prayers
and standing before the Lord; Those who pray:
Lord turn away from us the punishments of hell,
for it is a heavy torment, it is indeed an evil
dwelling place; Those who are neither
extravagant nor stingy in spending, but keep
a balance between the two; Those who repent
and believe and do good deeds.

Shinto Prayer for Peace

Although the people living across
the ocean surrounding us, I believe,
are all our brothers and sisters, why are
there constant troubles in this world?
Why do winds and waves rise in the ocean
surrounding us? I only earnestly wish
that the wind will soon puff away
all the clouds, which are hanging
over the tops of the mountains.

Prayer for Self-Control

REV. JOHN T. FARRELL

Source of Goodness, you know how often
I fail you by not exercising self-control and
by being unable to tame my caustic tongue.
Let me learn self-discipline and humility so that
I may cease speaking and writing sarcastic and
unkind words and expressing anger in my tone.
Let the goodness within my heart illuminate
my words, not the fear and anger that come from
my darker recesses. Let me dedicate my speech
to your service and to the service of others. May
I learn the value of silence, so I may not only
hear the voices of others, but your voice as well.

The Ethic of Reciprocity
Versions of the Golden Rule

Bahá'í Faith: Ascribe not to any soul that which you would not have ascribed to yourself, nor say not that which you do not. [Bahá'u'lláh]

Buddhism: Hurt not others in ways that you yourself would find hurtful. [Undana Varga 5:18]

Christianity: Therefore all things whatsoever ye would that men should do to you, do ye even so to them: for this is the law and the prophets. [Matthew 7:12, King James Version]

Confucism: Do not do to others what you do not want them to do to you. [Analects 15:23]

Ancient Egyptian: Do for one who may do for you, that you may cause him thus to do. [*The Tale of the Eloquent Peasant*, 109–110]

Hinduism: This is the sum of duty: do not do to others what would cause pain if done to you. [Mahabharata 5:1517]

Islam: None of you truly believes until he wishes
for his brother what he wishes for himself.
[Number 13 of *Imam Al-Nawawi's Forty Hadiths*]

Jainism: In happiness and suffering, in joy and grief,
we should regard all creatures as we regard our
own self. [Lord Mahavira, 24th Tirthankara]

Judaism: Thou shalt love thy neighbor
as thyself. [Leviticus 19:18]

Taoism: Regard your neighbor's gain as
your gain, and your neighbor's loss as your
own loss. [T'ai-Shang Kan-Ying P'ien]

Zoroastrianism: That nature alone is good
which refrains from doing another whatsoever
is not good for itself. [Dadisten-I-dinik, 94,5]

Be Generous in Prosperity

Be generous in prosperity,
And thankful in adversity.

Be fair in judgment,
And guarded in speech.

Be a lamp unto those,
Who walk in darkness.

Be eyes to the blind,
And a guiding light.

Be a breath of life,
To the body of mankind.

Be a dew to the soul
Of the human heart.

And a fruit upon the tree,
Of humanity.

From the *Writings of Bahá'u'lláh*

An Arrow Prayer for Times of Duress

REV. JOHN T. FARRELL

Breathing in: I love. . .
Breathing out: even my shadows.

Breathing in: I love. . .
Breathing out: even my enemies.

Peace Pilgrim's Beatitudes

PEACE PILGRIM

Blessed are they who give without expecting even thanks in return, for they shall be abundantly rewarded.

Blessed are they who translate every good thing they know into action, for ever higher truths shall be revealed unto them.

Blessed are they who do God's will without asking to see results, for great shall be their recompense.

Blessed are they who love and trust their fellow beings, for they shall reach the good in people and receive a loving response.

Blessed are they who have seen reality, for they know that not the garment of clay but that which activates the garment of clay is real and indestructible.

Blessed are those who see the change we call death as a liberation from the limitations of this earth-life, for they shall rejoice with their loved ones who make the glorious transition.

Blessed are they who after dedicating their lives and thereby receiving a blessing, have the courage and faith to surmount the difficulties of the path ahead, for they shall receive a second blessing.

Blessed are they who advance toward the spiritual path without the selfish motive of seeking inner peace, for they shall find it.

Blessed are they who instead of trying to batter down the gates of the kingdom of heaven approach them humbly and lovingly and purified, for they shall pass right through.

Used by permission. Peace Pilgrim. Compiled by some of her friends. *Peace Pilgrim: Her Life and Work in Her Own Words*, (Friends of Peace Pilgrim, 2004) pg. 167.

Prayers for Addicts

Two of the most important spiritual principles in recovery are compassion and empathy. Compassion, according to Thomas Merton, "is the keen awareness of the interdependence of all things."* Empathy describes our ability to share, identify, and understand the feelings of another person. Both of these principles are antidotes to the self-centeredness and self-indulgence that are symptomatic of the disease of addiction. The spiritual practice of compassion has been likened to opening the heart to the suffering and the joy of others. In recovery, we call this process of identification "the therapeutic value of one addict helping another"

---

* Thomas Merton quoted in *The Mystic Hours* by Wayne Teasdale

and claim it is "without parallel."[*] The practice of empathy begins when we allow ourselves to feel our own pain without numbing our feelings as we did in our active addiction. We learn to not turn away from pain but to move toward it with resolution and courage. Thus, we come to identify with other addicts in their distress and offer them solace and caring.

The prayers in this chapter run the gamut, beginning with two credos (statements of belief) written by recovering addicts. After that, there are prayers for addicts, for sponsors, for home groups, and for taking daily inventory. In recognition of diversity, there are prayers for women and for gays and lesbians and their friends. I also have included prayers for each of the Twelve Steps. The chapter concludes on a somber note with a prayer for the addicts we know who have left this life.

---

[*] Narcotics Anonymous, p. 18

A Recovering Addict's Credo I

REV. JOHN T. FARRELL

I believe in personal growth as intrinsic to my
recovery from addiction and personal dysfunction.

I believe connectedness is the most important
component of my spiritual life.

I believe that it is my ethical obligation to strive
for justice and peace among all people and to
respect the dignity of every human being.

I believe that I should love
my neighbor as myself.

I believe I should trust others and give
people the benefit of the doubt.

I believe that love is paramount,
and my relationships should be guided
by civility and respect.

I believe that hatred, incivility, bigotry, class
warfare, intimidation, and anger play no part in
recovery or in dialogue or in mature relationships.

I believe in freedom of expression.

I believe that I should speak out when
I happen upon hatred, incivility, bigotry,
class warfare, intimidation, and anger.

I believe that service to others is the
most noble of human endeavors.

I believe that most of what we call sin is the
result of fear and ignorance, but that it is not
a sin to be fearful and ignorant because all people
are educable and all fears can be overcome.

I believe that there are a few poor unfortunates
whom I can only help through prayer and by
avoiding personal contact with them.

A Recovering Addict's Credo II

LYNNE V

I believe I am an addict.

I believe in a power greater than myself
who loves me beyond all comprehension.

I believe God will often ask me to
step outside of my comfort zone.

I believe God has given me all the
gifts and graces I need.

I believe there is nothing to fear.

I believe God fills empty vessels with
riches beyond my imagination.

I believe those riches are mine for the asking.

I believe everyone is doing the
very best they can at all times.

I believe everyone in my life
is there for a reason.

I believe all of my struggles
begin and end with me.

I believe I take back my will
when I stop praying.

I believe my purpose is to serve
the people God puts in my life.

To the Spirit of Recovery

ST. AUGUSTINE

Breathe in me, O Holy Spirit,
that my thoughts may all be holy.

Act in me, O Holy Spirit,
that my work, too, may be holy.

Draw my heart, O Holy Spirit,
that I love but what is holy.

Strengthen me, O Holy Spirit,
to defend all that is holy.

Guard me, then, O Holy Spirit,
that I always may be holy. *Amen.*

Prayer for the Victims of Addiction

BOOK OF COMMON PRAYER

O blessed Lord, you ministered to all who
came to you: Look with compassion upon
all who through addiction have lost their health
and freedom. Restore to them the assurance
of your unfailing mercy; remove from them
the fears that beset them; strengthen them
in the work of their recovery; and to those
who care for them, give patient understanding
and persevering love. *Amen.*

A Twelfth-Step Prayer

God, your children are hungry.
They're lonely. They're cold. They're confused.
Don't let those of us in recovery walk by them
on the other side of the road. We get so caught
up in our own lives and our own so-called
"problems" that we forget there are people
who still suffer from the disease of addiction
in and out of the rooms. Open our eyes. Light
a fire under us so that we can do all we should do.
Help us give a hand up and not a hand out.
Help us show the world we are your children.
Help us show the world that the program is
a listening ear, an empathetic identification,
and a pathway to life. When we offer
ourselves to those in need, Lord, we
offer ourselves to you. *Amen.*

Adapted from the *Book of Prayer*

Meditation in Affliction

GYALWA LONGCHENPA

Assailed by afflictions,
we discover Dharma

And find the way to liberation.
Thank you, evil forces!

When sorrows invade the mind,
we discover Dharma

And find lasting happiness.
Thank you, sorrows!

Through harm caused by spirits
we discover Dharma

And find fearlessness.
Thank you, ghosts and demons!

Through people's hate
we discover Dharma

And find benefits and happiness.
Thank you, those who hate us!

Through cruel adversity,
we discover Dharma

And find the unchanging way.
Thank you, adversity!

Through being impelled to by others,
we discover Dharma

And find the essential meaning.
Thank you, all who drive us on!

We dedicate our merit to you all,
to repay your kindness.

A Sponsor's Prayer

REV. JOHN T. FARRELL

Help me to share my excitement about recovery,
my depth of spiritual connection, and
real examples of experience, strength, and hope.
In fact, help me to be a little more spiritual
while my sponsees are watching me.
Help me to share my knowledge about the steps,
my pride in my home group,
my openness to newcomers, and
my wrestling with life's perplexities.
Help me to accept the decisions my sponsees make.
As they are learning, guide me
in compassion and reason.
As they are growing, let me grow along with them.
When they grapple with questions,
let me avoid facile answers and clichés, and
whether I am a first-time sponsor or
have done this for thirty years,
Bring me with passion and humility to
seek your knowledge and will
for those you entrust to my care. *Amen.*

A Prayer for
My Home Group

REV. JOHN T. FARRELL

In the chaos and confusion of addiction,
let my home group gather together regularly
in hope, love, and fellowship, so that our
members may help ourselves by helping one
another. May we be messengers of recovery,
helping hands to suffering addicts, and a safe
haven for the distressed and discouraged. May
our meeting space be welcoming, may our
members be supportive and regular in their
attendance, and may our service be rooted
in spiritual principles. Keep our home group
safe, preserve it with love, and bless its
members with recovery. *Amen.*

A Daily Examen or Personal Inventory

ST. IGNATIUS OF LOYOLA

☙ Be aware of God's presence;

☙ Spend a moment looking over your day
with gratitude for this day's gifts;

☙ Ask God to send you the Spirit to help
you look at your actions, attitudes,
and motives with honesty and patience;

☙ Recall the events of your day;

☙ Have a heart-to-heart talk with God
as you look toward tomorrow.

Just for Today

Tell yourself:

Just for today my thoughts will be on my recovery,
living and enjoying life without the use of drugs.

Just for today I will have faith in someone
in NA who believes in me and wants to
help me in my recovery.

Just for today I will have a program.
I will try to follow it to the best of my ability.

Just for today, through NA, I will try to
get a better perspective on my life.

Just for today I will be unafraid.
My thoughts will be on my new associations,
people who are not using and who have
found a new way of life. So long as I follow
that way, I have nothing to fear.

Reprinted by permission of NA World Services, Inc.
All rights reserved.

Daily Inventory

REV. JOHN T. FARRELL

Am I making sufficient efforts to develop
my concept of a Higher Power?

How well have I sought to improve
my conscious contact with God?

Did I pray and meditate today?

When I was wrong, did I promptly admit it?

Was I in contact with another
recovering addict today?

Was I unkind or cruel to others,
sarcastic or caustic?

Did I nurture resentments?

Was I generous and patient with others?

Did I respect people around me,
especially those in authority and those
over whom I have authority?

Did I gossip maliciously and
detract from another's character?

Was I judgmental?

Did I express my displeasure by being
slow, sullen, and passive aggressive?

Did I exercise self-control
or was I angry and impatient?

Was I truthful and honest?

Was I a good friend?

Was I a good sponsor?

Was I grateful?

Was I a good example of recovery?

Will I do better tomorrow? How?

For All Women
A Litany

STACY CARMODY

For all women in our
community, nation, and world;

we pray to you, Lord God.

For all oppressed women;

grant them strength

to strive for equality,
freedom and justice.

Lord in your mercy
Hear our prayer.

For all women suffering abuse;

grant them full autonomy of body and mind.

Give every woman a healthy sense of self-worth
and confidence that does not cease.

Lord in your mercy
Hear our prayer.

Grant every woman infinite opportunity
in religious and secular life.

Give her means to ascend to
new heights and to break new ground.

Let her pathway be filled
with peace and dignity.

Lord in your mercy
Hear our prayer.

We remember those women who came before us.

We prepare for those we have yet to know.

Let our prayers be an inspiration to them,
now and forever. *Amen.*

For Those Who Hate Me, In and Out of the Rooms

REV. JOHN T. FARRELL

Source of Goodness, not everyone practices
the principles of love, acceptance, and
live-and-let-live you teach. Many are blinded
by unexamined prejudices and hatreds.
Some go out of their way to demean and
insult gay people. Others tacitly approve
of their behavior with silent complicity.

Some of this poison seeps into the rooms
of my fellowship and inhibits my recovery.
In my addiction, I felt like an orphan,
abandoned by father, mother, family, friends,
and society. I felt reviled and cursed. If this
kind of rejection happens in my recovery,
the joy of my heart will cease and I will be
alone in the wilderness again.

I pray for three things. First, that I will be
able to withstand prejudice when I encounter it
and find those who will offer me the love to
which all are entitled. Second, that I will be able
to stare hatred in the face and name it out loud,
for my sake, for the sake of other gay addicts,
and for the sake of the haters themselves.
And third, that I will try to understand and
forgive hateful behavior, knowing that I will
be forgiven only to the extent I can forgive.

I ask this in the name of the God
of justice and mercy. *Amen.*

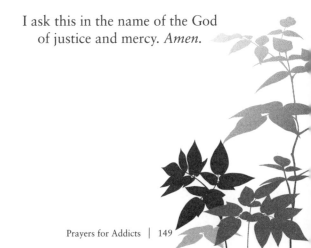

The Spirit of Truth

REV. JOHN T. FARRELL

Dear God, it is so easy to lie about who I am.
I've been doing it for so long. Since I first
understood the nature of sexuality, it seemed
easier to pretend I was something other than who
I was. I used all sorts of excuses—the effect of
my parents, the diminishment of my career, the
disapproval of my friends, my desire not to rock
the boat, a longing to please others, a need to play
athletics. I even believed that you God, my Creator
and Ground of my Being, wanted me to live a lie.

But there is a terrible cost in terms of stress,
pressure, and strain to living a lie. The more
I deny that I am gay, the more my self-hatred
expands. For so long, I didn't realize how the
negative energy of untruth was killing me.

Just for today, let me live my life in the spirit
of truth. My truth, God, is your truth, because
you created me. Let me be the embodiment
of your truth. Let me risk being who I am.
Let me make the truth sweet. May truth be
the cornerstone of my life in recovery.

A Prayer for Remembering Those Who Have Left This Life

In the rising of the sun and in its going down,
we remember them.

In the blowing of the wind and in the chill of the water,
we remember them.

In the opening of buds and in the rebirth of spring,
we remember them.

In the blueness of the sky and in the warmth of summer,
we remember them.

In the rustling of the leaves and in the beauty of autumn,
we remember them.

In the beginning of the year and when it ends,
we remember them.

When we are weary and in need of strength,
we remember them.

When we are lost and sick at heart,
we remember them.

When we have joys we yearn to share,
we remember them.

So long as we live, they too shall live,
for they are a part of us, *and we remember them.*

Amen.

Used by permission. Adapted from material originally produced by the National Episcopal AIDS Coalition and the Episcopal Church.

Prayers for the Twelve Steps

REV. JOHN T. FARRELL

First Step Prayer

I feel beaten into the ground. I am out of control,
and I have no power to manage my life. Help
me to see myself as I truly am and to admit that
I am suffering from the disease of addiction.

Second Step Prayer

My life is at the crossroads. One road seems
to lead to jails, institutions, and death. The other
leads to a new way of life. May I believe that my
life can be transformed and that my humanity
be restored by the road upon which I walk.

Third Step Prayer

I give myself to God to be used as God wishes.
May I be relieved of the bondage of self, so I may
better do God's will. May my fears, my selfishness,
and self-centeredness be taken away so I can be
an example to others of God's power, love,
and way of life. May I do God's will always.

Fourth Step Prayer

I have worn so many masks, made
so many mistakes, and hurt so many people
that learning about myself is a fearful task.
May I be relieved of my fears and be granted
the strength, courage, and honesty to take an
inventory of who I am and what I have done.

Fifth Step Prayer

Thank you for helping me find the ability
and bravery to look at myself clearly and honestly.
Thank you for the wisdom and guidance of
my sponsor throughout this step. Thank you
for the grace to lift the burden of guilt
and remorse from my heart.

Sixth Step Prayer

Grant me the readiness to ask God for
help in removing my defects of character.
May the spirit of honesty continue to help
me in recognizing the hidden corners of my life
that are still barriers to my recovery. May
I be guided toward wholeness and integrity.

Seventh Step Prayer

I pray for the humility to ask God to
remove my shortcomings. Give me an awareness
of who I am and what I need to grow in peace
and harmony with others. Through this step,
may I see not only my own dignity and worth,
but the dignity and worth of all.

Eighth Step Prayer

May I learn to stop regarding myself as
a victim of life and circumstance so that I can
enter fully into the spirit of this step. Let me
understand that I must only be concerned with
my behavior toward others, not with their
behavior toward me. May I be granted the
willingness to be forgiving and honest and to
always remember that the willingness to forgive
grows out of people's own need for forgiveness.

Ninth Step Prayer

For this step I will need strength, honesty,
and perseverance. Give me the understanding
that some amends may not just entail an apology,
but will require a genuine offer to make things
right. Guide me as I strive to change, not
just my behavior, but the person I was
when I came into recovery.

Tenth Step Prayer

Thank you for the honesty and insight I have
acquired through working the steps. Without them,
I would be unable to understand the necessity
for a daily inventory. Thank you also for the
strength to admit I am wrong on occasion. That
ability will diminish the self-righteousness and
denial that are so much a part of my disease.

Eleventh Step Prayer

Help me understand the meaning and value
of prayer so I may improve my conscious contact
with the spiritual forces underlying my recovery.
May I be granted the silence and space that are
necessary for meditation so I can hear the small,
still voice of the divine within me.

Twelfth Step Prayer

Dear God, it is said that "faith without works is
dead." I thank you for the recovery I have been
given through the spiritual experience of working
the steps. I understand that this gift is not mine
alone and that it is my duty and my joy to share
the message of recovery with all who suffer and to
help all who ask my aid. Give me the desire to help
others and to practice the spiritual principles of
recovery all the days of my life, one day at a time.

Prayers of Gratitude

Acrucial tool in the recovery process is the spiritual principle of gratitude. So often the disease of addiction encourages us to focus on the negative, on our complaints, and on our entitlements. Gratitude reverses that process. Being grateful for what we have is vital to our quest to live for today and embrace life in the here and now. Prayers of gratitude play a part in our growth. They help us to see life as it is and to stop identifying ourselves as victims. Even in recovery we still encounter a world where the perception of lack and scarcity drives our fears.

Being thankful for our blessings enhances our recovery and makes us better equipped to encounter the world as an enjoyable place. No one likes a complainer or someone who feels entitled. In recovery, our spiritual condition grows when we count our blessings. We can enrich our daily lives if we impart blessings and express our gratitude to all we encounter. We can even do this anonymously. Try this one day: in a public place such as a bus or a restaurant or at a meeting, focus on a stranger and silently bless the person, "May serenity and joy enter your life." You may even use your own blessing. See how you feel afterwards. By blessing others, we become blessed ourselves.

The prayers in this chapter include texts written by medieval saints, thoughts from an eighteenth century philosopher, and a favorite twentieth century poem. All express gratitude and joy in life.

Buddhist Mealtime Prayer

This food is the gift of the whole universe,

Each morsel is a sacrifice of life,

May I be worthy to receive it.

May the energy in this food,

Give me the strength,

To transform my unwholesome
qualities into wholesome ones.

I am grateful for this food,

May I realize the Path of Awakening,

For the sake of all beings.

Namo Amida Buddha.

Day by Day

ST. RICHARD OF CHICHESTER

Thanks be to Thee, my Lord Jesus Christ,
for all the benefits thou hast given me,

for all the pains and insults
thou hast borne for me.

O most merciful redeemer,
friend, and brother,
may I know Thee more clearly,
love Thee more dearly,
and follow Thee more nearly,
day by day. *Amen.*

Bring Me Home to Thy Fold

ST. JEROME

O good shepherd, seek me out,
and bring me home to thy fold again.

Deal favorably with me
according to thy good pleasure,

Till I may dwell in thy house
all the days of my life,

And praise thee for ever and
ever with them that are there.

The Palace of Wisdom

EMANUEL SWEDENBORG

Picture wisdom as a magnificent
and finely decorated palace. One climbs
up to enter this palace by twelve steps.
One can only arrive at the first step by means
of the Lord's power through joining with Him. . .

As a person climbs these steps,
he perceives that
no one is wise from himself
but from the Lord. . .

The twelve steps into the palace
of wisdom signify love in union
with faith and faith in union with love.

The Canticle of the Creatures

ST. FRANCIS OF ASSISI

Most High, all-powerful, all-good Lord,
All praise is Yours, all glory, honor and blessings.
To you alone, Most High, do they belong;
No mortal lips are worthy to pronounce Your Name.

We praise You, Lord, for all Your creatures,
Especially for Brother Sun,
Who is the day through whom You give us light.
And he is beautiful and radiant with great splendor,
Of You Most High, he bears your likeness.

We praise You, Lord, for Sister Moon and the stars,
In the heavens you have made them
bright, precious and fair.

We praise You, Lord, for Brothers Wind and Air,
Fair and stormy, all weather's moods,
By which You cherish all that You have made.

We praise You, Lord, for Sister Water,
So useful, humble, precious and pure.

We praise You, Lord, for Brother Fire,
Through whom You light the night.
He is beautiful, playful, robust and strong.

We praise You, Lord, for Sister Earth,
Who sustains us
With her fruits, colored flowers, and herbs.

We praise You, Lord, for those who pardon,
For love of You bear sickness and trial.
Blessed are those who endure in peace,
By You Most High, they will be crowned.

We praise You, Lord, for Sister Death,
From whom no one living can escape.
Woe to those who die in their sins!
Blessed are those that she finds
doing Your Will.
No second death can do them harm.

We praise and bless You, Lord,
and give You thanks,
And serve You in all humility.

Count Your Blessings!

AUTHOR UNKNOWN

Count your blessings instead of your crosses;
Count your gains instead of your losses.

Count your joys instead of your woes;
Count your friends instead of your foes.

Count your laughs instead of your tears;
Count your courage instead of your fears.

Count your full years instead of your lean;
Count your kind deeds instead of your mean.

Count your health instead of your wealth;
Count on God instead of yourself.

To Thank You, Lord,
For Hearing All My Prayers

REV. BILL MCGINNIS

I thank you, Lord, for hearing all my prayers,

For taking time to listen to my pleas,

For taking action, when you thought it best,

And for withholding, when the time was wrong.

As shepherd to his sheep, You are to me,

And I am happy being in Your fold. *Amen.*

Doxology

JOSEPHINE DELPHINE
HENDERSON HEARD

Great God accept our gratitude,
For the great gifts on us bestowed—
For raiment, shelter, and for food.
Great God, our gratitude we bring,
Accept our humble offering,
For all the gifts on us bestowed,
Thy name be evermore adored.

Prayers for Spiritual Connection

Connectedness is *the* operative principle we seek to infuse into our spiritual lives. In recovery, we cast off the isolation of addiction and learn that everything and everyone in life and creation are interconnected. No one is entirely alone. Our personal stories weave into the stories of others. Life linked to life reveals one global condition. All seem connected to a power greater than ourselves who is the "Hidden Ground of Love,"* the name Thomas Merton coined for the Spirit that governs creation and inspires us to seek goodness in all things and all people. No one exists outside the grid of humanity.

* Thomas Merton quoted in Wm. Shannon, *The Hidden Ground of Love*.

Our recognition and acceptance of our connectedness reduces our feelings of alienation and apartness. Our experience of connectedness increases our sense of joy and love of life.

The prayers in this chapter are mostly modern, and several of them were written by people in recovery. Some of these prayers, especially the one by Swami Akhilananda of Bangladesh, recognize the universality of humanity in our desire to connect to the numinous. A connection to the divine is seeing the divine both as a good thing in itself and as a way of connecting with each other. The one exception to these modern efforts is the prayer written by Ambrose of Milan from the fourth century, which is a way of reminding us of how ancient the quest for connection is.

The Knots Prayer

AUTHOR UNKNOWN

Dear God,
Please untie the knots
That are in my mind,
My heart and my life.
Remove the have nots,
The can nots and the do nots
That I have in my mind.

Erase the will nots,
May nots, and
Might nots that find
A home in my heart.

Release me from the could nots,
Would nots, and
Should nots that obstruct my life.

And most of all, dear God,
I ask that you remove from my mind
My heart and my life all of the am nots
That I have allowed to hold me back,
Especially the thought
That I am not good enough.

A Prayer of Connection

REV. JOHN T. FARRELL

Source of Being, most of my life is focused
on myself and the people I know, the places
I visit, and the things I encounter. But, even
in my most mundane encounters and moments,
if I listen carefully or if I pause for just a second,
I can hear your small, still voice and sense your
presence around and within me. Help me
recognize those moments of connection amidst
the "busy-ness" and distractions of my life.
Let me cherish and be nourished by your
loving presence in my life, in the lives
of those whom I meet, and in the life
of the world around me. *Amen.*

A Prayer for God's Presence

GREG P *(NA MEMBER)*

Dear God, protect me and provide for me.

Guide me and illuminate the path of my pilgrimage.

Grant me courage, commitment, and strength.

Teach me to care and give without reservation.

Make me aware of gratitude and principle.

Help me recognize your presence around me.

And let my life be a reflection of your love. *Amen.*

To the God of All

SWAMI AKHILANANDA

May He who is the Father in Heaven of the Christians, Holy One of the Jews, Allah of the Muhammadans, Buddha of the Buddhists, Tao of the Chinese, Ahura Mazda of the Zoroastrians, and Brahman of the Hindus lead us from the unreal to the real, from darkness to light, from disease and death to immortality. May the All-Loving Being manifest Himself unto us, and grant us abiding understanding and all-consuming divine love. Peace, Peace. Peace be unto all.

Used by permission of Vedanta Society of Providence.

Spiritual Perfection

"Be ye perfect, even as your Father which is in
heaven is perfect." The soul, remaining in its
disorderly will, is imperfect; it becomes more
perfect, in proportion as it approaches nearer to
the Divine will. When a soul is advanced so far
that it cannot in anything depart there from, it
then becomes wholly perfect, united with, and is
transformed into, the divine nature; and being thus
purified and united to Infinite Purity, it finds
a profound peace, and a sweet rest, which brings
it to such a perfect union of love, that it is filled
with joy. It conforms itself to the will of the
great Original in all emergencies, and rejoiced in
everything to do the divine good pleasure.

Adapted from *A Guide to True Peace, or A Method
of Attaining to Inward and Spiritual Prayer*

I Only Know
What I Need, Lord

FRANÇOIS DE SALIGNAC DE LA
MOTHE-FÉNELON, ARCHBISHOP OF CAMBRAY

Lord, I know not what I ought to ask of Thee;

Thou only knowest what I need;
Thou lovest me better

Than I know how to love myself.
O Father, give to Thy

Child that which he himself knows not how to ask.

I dare not ask either for crosses or for consolations;

I simply present myself before Thee,

I open my heart to Thee. Behold my needs

Which I know not myself; see and do according to

Thy tender mercy. Smite, or heal; depress me,

Or raise me up; I adore all Thy purposes without

Knowing them; I am silent; I offer myself in

Sacrifice; I yield myself to Thee; I would have

No other desire than to accomplish Thy will.

Teach me to pray. Pray Thyself in me. *Amen.*

A Prayer for Seeking God

ST. AMBROSE OF MILAN

O Lord, teach me to seek you, and
reveal yourself to me when I seek you.
For I cannot seek you unless you first
teach me, not find you unless you first reveal
yourself to me. Let me seek you in longing,
and long for you in seeking. Let me find
you in love, and love you in finding.

Outside My Window

MACRINA WIEDERKEHR

There's a poem outside my window
that refuses to be written down.
Having no need to be published,
It desires rather to be taken in,
Utterly received, tenderly integrated,
lovingly included in my life.

It summons me
to behold it in silence,
cradle its healing graces,
enjoy its magical aura,
keep it secret
except for those
who notice it on their own.

It does not wish
to be proclaimed, named or analyzed.
It desires rather to be slowly revealed,
honored and absorbed.
As it shyly releases its energy
it wants to enchant me, entrance me,
drawing me into the miracle
of being in the quiet
mystery of its company.

Look out your window!
There's a poem waiting for you too.

Used by permission of Wiederkehr OSB, Macrina.
"Outside My Window." Joyful Gifts. Charleston,
South Carolina. Create Space, 2010.89.

Unclench My Fist, God

HENRI NOUWEN

Dear God, I am so afraid
to open my clenched fists!

Who will I be when I have
nothing left to hold on to?

Who will I be when I stand
before you with empty hands?

Please help me to
gradually open my hands

and to discover that
I am not what I own,

but what you want to give me.

And what you want
to give me is love—

unconditional,
everlasting love. *Amen.*

Excerpted from *With Open Hands* by Henri J. M. Nouwen.

Copyright © 1972, 1995, 2005 by Ave Maria Press,
PO Box 428, Notre Dame, IN 46556, www.avemariapress.com.
Used with permission of the publisher.

God Speaks to Me

MICHAEL HIGGINS

With sign and wonder
With song and thunder
God speaks to me.

With pain and joy
With color and in another
God speaks to me.

My heart, my soul
And mind, this podium
Be.

His fire burns my lips,
With my voice He sings.
All around, all around.

Like a melody playing,
God speaks.
God speaks,
God speaks,
To me!

When You're Angry at God

Psalm 10:1

Why, O Lord, do you stand far off?

Why do you hide yourself in times of trouble?

Psalm 22:1

My God, my God, why have you forsaken me?

Why are you so far from saving me,

So far from the words of my groaning?

Psalm 42:9

I say to God my Rock,

"Why have you forgotten me?

Why must I go about mourning,

Oppressed by the enemy?"

Psalm 44:23-24

Awake, O Lord! Why do you sleep?

Rouse yourself! Do not reject us forever.

Why do you hide your face

And forget our misery and oppression?

Psalm 74:1

Why have you rejected us forever, O God?

Why does your anger smolder against
the sheep of your pasture?

Psalm 74:11

Why do you hold back your hand,
your right hand?

Take it from the folds of your
garment and destroy them!

Psalm 79:10

Why should the nations say,

"Where is their God?"

Before our eyes,
make known among the nations

That you avenge the outpoured
blood of your servants.

To Avoid Carelessness

REV. BILL MCGINNIS

Sometimes when you are busy with your life,
And jumping frantically from place to place
It's easy to forget about details,
Like where you put your keys or left your coat,
Or if your backup copy has been made.
And so I pray the Lord will stay with you
And warn you when you walk in carelessness.
I pray that He protects you from the harm
That careless actions easily produce.

Evening Prayers

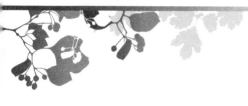

Prayer has been described as "the breath of the soul."* During the day we breathe in the joy and challenge of our lives in recovery. We work, we play, we interact, we love, we quarrel, and we may even help another person or two. But, for most of us, the habit of conscious prayer is not something we make time for as we go about our daily lives. No matter, bidden or not, God is present anyway. In the evening, however, it is different. The day is over, we can relax, and we are at rest. This is the moment to connect with God in prayer and to let our souls take a breath before we sleep. Now is the time for prayer. I have discovered an unexpected spiritual bonus in my evening prayers. Not only do I feel connected

---

* *The Breath of the Soul: Reflections on Prayer* by Joan Chittister.

to God, I feel connected to those in recovery who may be praying at the same time. As I finish the holy practice of evening prayer, I often have an awareness that as I say my final *amen*, I am handing over my prayers to my fellow addicts praying in the next time zone. Thus, I feel like a relay runner passing a torch in a continuous turning over of lives and wills to the care of God as we understand God.

The prayers in this chapter include prayers from the Christian, Jewish, and Celtic spiritual traditions. There are several versions of the Lord's Prayer. Several are called "Compline Prayers." *Compline* is a term used by monks to describe their final prayers of the day. The word is derived from the Latin *completorium*, as Compline is the completion of the working day.

A Celtic Evening Prayer

God to enfold me,
God to surround me,
God in my speaking,
God in my thinking.
God in my sleeping,
God in my waking,
God in my watching,
God in my hoping.
God in my life,
God in my lips,
God in my soul,
God in my heart.
God in my sufficing,
God in my slumber,
God in mine ever-living soul,
God in mine eternity. *Amen.*

From the *Carmina Gadelica*

Prayer for Sleep

REV. JOHN T. FARRELL

I cry out for help this night to ask that
my fears be relieved. Fear holds me back
from accomplishing the goals I hold dear
and my worry and anxiety increase. Sleep
is sometimes hard and the terrors of night
keep me awake. May I be soothed by
gentleness and may my mind and heart
be calmed. May I lay my burdens down
at God's feet and get a good
night's rest. *Amen.*

Finish Every Day

RALPH WALDO EMERSON

Finish every day and be done with it.
You have done what you could.
Some blunders and absurdities
no doubt have crept in;
forget them as soon as you can.

Tomorrow is a new day;
begin it well and serenely
and with too high a spirit
to be cumbered with
your old nonsense.

This day is all that is
good and fair.
It is too dear,
with its hopes and invitations,
to waste a moment on yesterdays.

The Lord's Prayer
Traditional Version

Our Father, who art in Heaven,

Hallowed be thy name;

Thy kingdom come,

Thy will be done,

On earth, as it is in heaven.

Give us this day our daily bread;

And forgive us our trespasses

As we have forgiven those
who trespass against us;

And lead us not into temptation,

But deliver us from evil.

For thine is the kingdom,

And the power,

And the glory,

Forever and ever. *Amen.*

The Lord's Prayer
Modern Version
BOOK OF COMMON PRAYER

Our Father in heaven,
Hallowed be your Name,
Your kingdom come,
Your will be done,
On earth as in heaven.
Give us today our daily bread.
Forgive us our sins
As we forgive those
Who sin against us.
Save us from the time of trial,
And deliver us from evil.
For the kingdom, the power,
And the glory are yours,
Now and for ever. *Amen.*

The Lord's Prayer
Alternate Version

GLENDA GREEN

Our Father who is innocent and pure,

Holy is your name.

May love be seen as all that it is.

May earth be seen as heaven is.

Nourish this day with your bountiful supply,

And allow us to receive as

We give that right to others.

Restore us from the perils of illusion,

And renew our perception of truth.

For truth is the kingdom,

And love is the power,

And Yours is the glory forever.

Compline Prayer I

ST. AUGUSTINE

Watch, O Lord, with those who wake, or
Watch, or weep tonight, and give your angels
And saints charge over those who sleep.
Tend your sick ones, O Lord.
Rest your weary ones,
Bless your dying ones,
Soothe your suffering ones,
Pity your afflicted ones,
Shield your joyous ones,
And all for your love's sake. *Amen.*

Compline Prayer II

REV. JOHN T. FARRELL

Sometimes life lays a gentle yoke upon
me and other times just getting through
the day is a burden. But nothing I endure
is more than I can handle. Your presence
gives me strength; your spirit gives me endurance;
and your love enfolds me. Receive the work
and the prayers I have offered to you today.
And now, give me rest and a good night's sleep,
so tomorrow I will be all the more eager to serve
you and follow the path of recovery. *Amen.*

Compline Prayer III

BOOK OF COMMON PRAYER

Be present, O merciful God, and
protect us through the hours of this night,
so that we who are wearied by the changes
and chances of this life may rest in your
eternal changelessness. *Amen.*

A Nighttime Prayer

REV. JOHN T. FARRELL

I believe that God is watching. The Gospel of Luke says, "Are not five sparrows sold for two pennies? Yet not one of them is forgotten by God. Indeed, the very hairs of your head are all numbered. Don't be afraid; you are worth more than many sparrows." When God watches me during the day, I want him to see compassion, joy, and a spirit of service to others. I want to be a good friend, a loving companion, and a worker among workers. And if I have not been these things, I know God will forgive me. Tomorrow is another day and I pray that I will be better at doing these things. But I shall always be the apple of God's eye and for that I am grateful. *Amen.*

A Bedtime Prayer

REV. JOHN T. FARRELL

Now I lay me down to sleep.

I pray my Higher Power
my soul to keep.

May my recovery grow
through the night,

And keep me safe
until morning light.

The Last Word

JOHN 14:1-3

Let not your hearts be troubled;
believe in God, believe also in me.
In my Father's house are many rooms;
if it were not so, would I have told you
that I go to prepare a place for you?
And when I go and prepare a place for you,
I will come again and will take you to myself,
that where I am you may be also.

Books for Your Spiritual Journey

Holy Silence: The Gift of Quaker Spirituality by J. Brent Bell (Paraclete Press)

Of Character: Building Assets in Recovery by Denise Crosson (Central Recovery Press)

The Celtic Vision: Prayers, Blessings, Songs, and Invocations from the Gaelic Tradition by Esther de Waal (Liguori/Triumph)

Lost in Wonder: Rediscovering the Spiritual Art of Attentiveness by Esther de Waal (Liturgical Press)

Simply SoulStirring: Writing as a Meditative Practice by Francis Dorff (Paulist Press)

Father Mychal Judge: An Authentic American Hero by Michael Ford (Paulist Press)

Coming Out to God: Prayers for Lesbians and Gay Men, Their Families, and Friends by Chris Glaser (Presbyterian Publishing Corp.)

Reformation of the Heart: Seasonal Meditations by a Gay Christian by Chris Glaser (Westminster/John Knox Press)

A 12-Step Approach to the Spiritual Exercises of St. Ignatius by Jim Harbaugh (Sheed & Ward)

The Heart of the Qur'an: An Introduction to Islamic Spirituality by Lex Hixon and Neil Douglas-Klotz (Quest Books)

A Child in Winter: Advent, Christmas, and Epiphany with Caryll Houselander by Caryll Houselander and Thomas Hoffman (Sheed & Ward)

Against the Stream: A Buddhist Manual for Spiritual Revolutionaries by Noah Levine, (HarperOne)

The Wisdom of the Desert by Thomas Merton (New Directions)

The Wounded Healer: Ministry in Contemporary Society by Henri Nouwen (Image)

Love's Redeeming Work: The Anglican Quest for Holiness by Geoffrey Rowell, Kenneth Stevenson, and Rowan Williams (Oxford University Press)

Everyday Simplicity: A Practical Guide to Spiritual Growth by Robert Wicks (Sorin Books)

Seven Sacred Pauses: Living Mindfully Through the Hours of the Day by Macrina Wiederkehr (Sorin Books)